Pebble®
Plus

T0077117

Nocturnal Animals

by Abbie Dunne

CAPSTONE PRESS
a capstone imprint

Pebble Plus is published by Capstone Press,
1710 Roe Crest Drive, North Mankato, Minnesota 56003
www.mycapstone.com

Library of Congress Cataloging-in-Publication Data
Names: Dunne, Abbie, author.
Title: Nocturnal animals / by Abbie Dunne.
Description: North Mankato, Minnesota : Capstone Press, [2017] | Series:
   Pebble plus. Life science | Audience: Ages 4-8.? | Audience: K to grade
   3.? | Includes bibliographical references and index.
Identifiers: LCCN 2016005319| ISBN 9781515709466 (library binding) | ISBN
   9781515709787 (pbk.) | ISBN 9781515711131 (ebook pdf)
Subjects: LCSH: Nocturnal animals--Juvenile literature. | Animal
   behavior--Juvenile literature.
Classification: LCC QL755.5 .D86 2017 | DDC 591.5/18--dc23
LC record available at http://lccn.loc.gov/2016005319

Editorial Credits
Linda Staniford, editor; Bobbie Nuytten, designer; Jo Miller, media researcher;
Tori Abraham, production specialist

Photo Credits
Newscom: Photoshot/NHPA/Javier Alonso Huerta, 17, Photoshot/NHPA/Stephen Dalton, 1, 15; Shutterstock: ARENA Creative, 19, colin robert varndell, 11, Dirk Ercken, cover (front), 7, EcoPrint, 5, IMAGE LAGOON, 21, Joe Gough, 20, Robert Hardholt, 13, Yanik Chauvin, 9, Zygomatic, cover (back)

Design Elements
Shutterstock: Alena P

Note to Parents and Teachers

The Life Science set supports national curriculum standards for science. This book introduces the concept of nocturnal animals. The images support early readers in understanding the text. The repetition of words and phrases helps early readers in understanding the text. This book also introduces early readers to subject-specific vocabulary words, which are defined in the Glossary section. Early readers may need assistance to read some words and to use the Table of Contents, Glossary, Read More, Internet Sites, Critical Thinking Using the Common Core, and Index sections of the book.

Printed in the United States   6043

Table of Contents

Night Life

There is a busy world
when the sun goes down.
At night nocturnal animals
are on the go. They have
adapted to life in darkness.

Night Senses

Nocturnal animals see well in darkness. Frogs use their bulging eyes to spot insects. Their night sight also helps them leap between tree branches.

Nocturnal animals use their sense of smell to help them in the dark. Foxes track prey with their noses.

Nocturnal animals have good hearing. Owls can hear prey from far away. Large ears help mice hear sneaky predators.

Eating at Night

Hungry nocturnal animals come out at night to eat. The darkness helps tigers and leopards hide. They quietly sneak up on prey.

Bats use echolocation to find food in darkness. They make noises and listen for echoes. Large ears help them find prey.

Most owls hunt for food
at night. Large eyes
help them spot small
animals in the darkness.

Day Sleepers

Nocturnal animals

sleep during the day.

Bats hang out in caves.

Foxes live inside dark dens.

Owls sleep in barns or trees.

Activity

How do nocturnal animals use their senses to help them move, find food, and eat? Find out!

What You Need

- blindfold (handkerchief or sleep mask)
- fruit
- music

What You Do

1. Put on a blindfold.

2. Pick up the fruit and smell.

3. Remove the blindfold. Smell the fruit again.

4. Did you smell it better with or without the blindfold?

5. Put the blindfold on again.

6. This time bite into the fruit and chew slowly.

7. Remove the blindfold and take another bite. Chew slowly.

8. Did it taste different? Was it better with or without the blindfold?

9. Listen to a song with the blindfold on.

10. Now listen to the same song without the blindfold.

11. Did you notice a difference? Could you hear it better with or without the blindfold?

What Do You Think?

Make a claim about nocturnal animals.

How do senses help nocturnal animals?

Use facts from your test to support your claim.

Glossary

adapt—to change to better fit into a new or different environment

echolocation—the process of using sounds and echoes to locate objects; bats use echolocation to find food

insect—a small animal with a hard outer shell, six legs, three body sections, and two antennae; most insects have wings

nocturnal—active at night and resting during the day

predator—an animal that hunts other animals for food

prey—an animal hunted by another animal for food

senses—seeing, hearing, tasting, smelling and touching; using our senses helps us learn about our surroundings

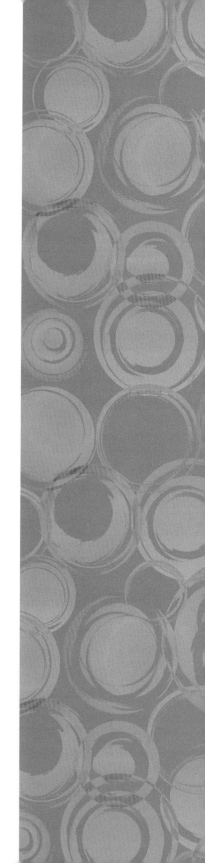

Read More

Hicks, Kelli L. *Nocturnal Animals*. Learn About Animal Behavior. North Mankato, Minn.: Capstone Press, 2013.

Bodden, Valerie. *Owls*. Amazing Animals. North Mankato, MN: Creative Education, 2013.

Rabe, Tish. *Out of Sight Till Tonight! All About Nocturnal Animals.* The Cat in the Hat's Learning Library. New York: Random House, 2015.

Internet Sites

FactHound offers a safe, fun way to find Internet sites related to this book. All of the sites on FactHound have been researched by our staff.

Here's all you do:

Visit *www.facthound.com*

Type in this code: 9781515709466

Super-cool stuff! Check out projects, games and lots more at **www.capstonekids.com**

Critical Thinking Using the Common Core

1. Nocturnal animals hunt at night. Which senses are adapted to help them do this? (Key Ideas and Details)

2. Bats hunt for food using echolocation. Explain what this means. (Key Ideas and Details)

3. Why do you think nocturnal animals sleep during the day? (Integration of Knowledge and Ideas)

4. Mice have large ears and very good hearing. How do you think this helps them? (Integration of Knowledge and Ideas)

Index